Trauma to Transformed

Uncovering the Gems Within

Based on a True Story

Charlotte Twycross

Copyright

Copyright © 2025

Trauma to Transformed: Uncovering the Gems Within by **Charlotte Twycross**

ALL RIGHTS RESERVED. No part of this book may be reproduced in any form, stored in a retrieval system, or transmitted in any form by any means – electronic, mechanical, photocopy, recording, or otherwise – without the author and publisher's prior written permission, except in brief reviews.

This fictional work is based on a true story. Names, characters, places, and incidents are either the product of the author's imagination or are used fictitiously for identity protection. Any resemblance to actual persons, living or dead, events, locales and characteristics are entirely coincidental.

Disclaimer: This book contains some sensitive events and discussions suited for adults and counsellors.

The Bible Scripture is taken from the New King James Version®. Copyright © 1982 by Thomas Nelson. Used by permission. All rights reserved.

Book formatting and editing: Dr Jacqueline N Samuels

https://tinyurl.com/AuthorJNSamuels

ISBN: **9798317257248**

Table of Contents

Copyright	iii
Acknowledgements	vii
Dedication	viii
Foreword	ix
Endorsements	xi
Preface	xvii
Introduction	xix
Part One	1
Chapter One: Meet Charlotte	2
Chapter Two: Twisted Teens	17
Chapter Three: Ripple Effect of my Parents' Lifestyles	21
Chapter Four: Two-Faced Parenting	27
Chapter Five: Supporting Children Through Challenges	31
Part Two	35
Chapter Six: Trauma Triggers	36
Chapter Seven: The Healing Journey	41
Chapter Eight: Reclaim Your Power and Self-Esteem	48
Part Three	53
Chapter Nine: Destiny Helpers	54
Chapter Ten: Growth And Development	59
Chapter Eleven: Sharing Our Lived Experiences	65
Chapter Twelve: Healing Prayers	71
Chapter Thirteen: Morning Devotion and Gratitude Affirmations	78
Chapter Fourteen: Emotional Healing Quotes	86
Chapter Fifteen: Navigating Life's Purpose	89
Useful Resources for Support	92
Conclusion	100
About The Author	102
References	103

Acknowledgements

I wish to thank and acknowledge the following wonderful people who have contributed immensely to my journey and growth.

Pastor Jacob, my first pastor who guided me into salvation, forgiveness and love.

Pastor Joselyn Myers, my mentor and prayer warrior for uplifting me and being on hand for constant encouragement.

Fitness Coach Martha, for your guidance in my emotional and spiritual growth.

Pastor Isabel Austin for spiritual uplifting and introducing me to my book publishing coach and mentor, Dr Jane Ellis.

Tabby, my confidant, who introduced me to the initial book outline and a mentor in this writing journey.

To Pippa, my anchor whose heart inspires my life and family.

My wonderful children who have lovingly supported me with positive energy and understanding.

All your unique contributions have synchronised perfectly and inspired my writing and creativity.

Dedication

I dedicate this book to my children Bella, Ray, Mia and Sarah. You are my everything.

You have been my deepest encouragement to keep going. May my life inspire you to be all you are called to be.

Foreword

Born into a family, raised in France, growing up, getting married, and having children—all this sounds like the ideal progression in life. Yet, the stories within these pages reveal a journey far from ideal, marked by pain, trauma, and unimaginable abuse. Despite all this, the author has remained standing.

As a pastor, I've encountered many people with stories of suffering and survival. Some have endured trauma so deep that you wonder how they continue to stand, how they keep smiling, giving, and loving. This book tells such a story—a journey from pain and discouragement to triumph.

I've known the author for many years, and from the outside, you'd never guess the depth of what she's endured. You might ask yourself: *How does she keep going?* The answer is clear—God has graced her with strength, faith, and favour, covering her with His love. Charlotte stands as a witness of what the grace of God can do, carrying her through pain and trials, and emerging with a story beautified by His love.

As you read this book, may these experiences empower you to support, love, and walk with others through their struggles. This is a true story of God's grace, carrying the author through childhood trauma, major diagnoses, surgeries, and a life-threatening accident.

Yet, by God's mercy, her story was far from over. Psalm 89:13 reminds us that His hand was upon her.

May you be inspired and empowered as you dive into Charlotte's testimony of moving from trauma to triumph, ill health to healing, brokenness to wholeness, and sorrow to joy—a story of God's grace transforming a life so that it no longer looks like what it has been through.

Pastor Isabel Austin

Endorsements

I met Charlotte at work in Morocco. We grew from work colleagues to best buddies and have kept in touch over the years as our lives have taken us to different parts of the world.

Charlotte's continual growth has evolved as she has mastered a very stressful job where we were both thrown into the deep end. She played her wife-mother role admirably despite inadequate support and navigated life in a foreign country with no immediate family nearby. Somehow Charlotte masterfully kept it all together.

The author's unwavering resilience throughout life's transitions has deeply inspired me. Since courageously returning to France Charlotte's career continues to grow. She has regained her footing, found her voice, established her independence and grown against all odds.

When Charlotte mentioned her intention to write her book I was most excited because I knew her story would encourage other women to find their voice and way.

I have since trained as a life coach, and every time we have a session together, I am in awe of how willing she is to grow as an individual and look forward to witnessing her story unfold.

Zoe Molu

As a mother, grandmother and Pastor, some of my responsibilities include supporting individuals going through difficulties and normal challenges in life. I also coordinate monthly prayer meetings where we all meet to worship and pray to God.

When Charlotte attended her first meeting she listened attentively as we shared about the effects of toxic soul ties and relationships. We touched on the damaging effects of sexual relationships both mentally and emotionally if they were not well managed.

Shortly after Charlotte made an appointment to see me privately noting that most of what I said during the teachings touched on her own life. She looked fearful and desperate for answers. She was feeling broken, helpless, hopeless, and traumatized by her past and ongoing experiences. I encouraged her that as God intervened in her situation, she had a bigger role to extricate herself from the trauma.

Charlotte keenly actioned every instruction with the Holy Spirit's guidance. She was very obedient and never missed her appointments. She was bold, courageous and determined to get herself out of her status quo to be a new empowered person physically, socially, spiritually, emotionally, mentally and financially. She started looking for a counsellor and a job, joined the gym to lose weight, found a better house to live in and stepped into the community to support others.

Identifying her weaknesses as stepping stones, she turned her pain to gain and mess to a message of hope for other hurting souls seeking inner lasting restoration.

Initially Charlotte phoned me three times a day; this reduced to calling me when necessary. God has transformed her into a loving, kind, friendly and empathetic woman who values herself, her family, the community, church and this nation. She has become a trailblazer who epitomises courage and hope among her peers and especially those who know her journey.

She is the person described in Job 14:7-9, *At least there is hope for a tree: If it is cut down, it will sprout again, and its new shoots will not fail. Its roots may grow old in the ground and its stump die in the soil, yet at the scent of water it will bud and put forth shoots like a plant.*

She birthed her intention to write a book during one of our meetings. We agreed that in addition to helping heal her wounded past, her story would support and encourage others who have experienced similar situations.

Charlotte's work would also leave a legacy for generations. I am proud of the loving and innocent woman Charlotte is. The author is also a great pillar for her children, family and church. I wish her well in all her endeavours and a long life filled health, wealth and honour.

Her pastor, sister, prayer partner and mentor.

Pastor Becky Skinner

Charlotte and I met when our children attended the same nursery school. We bonded immediately. The first thing that struck me was how intentional she was. With three young children at the time, she was fully focused on their education and wellbeing, keen to enable them to achieve their best. I was star struck by her energy and capacity.

Our friendship grew very quickly and in a short time, she became my sister. I have watched and experienced Charlotte go through various stages; at each stage I have continued to be in awe of her capacity to remain kind and good and push through it all.

Charlotte's story demonstrates inner strength, persistence, love and most importantly, God's handiwork. She is an extraordinary human being, a highly intelligent woman, a formidable mother, the kindest and most compassionate friend. This story will inspire many and I can't wait to see the great impact this will have on humanity and more specifically women.

Charlotte is a phenomenal woman.

Amanda G

Throughout my lifetime Charlotte has been an amazing support system as my eldest sister, confidante and first best friend. As a young child I looked up to Charlotte and she was a second mother to me, helping me bathe, dress and prancing me about on her back. I always held her in high regard; she was in my eyes so beautiful, radiant and bright. I always knew she was way more than this however. Even in the early years her caring nature would shine through along with her deep sense of responsibility.

Faced with exams I remember seeing my sister crumble momentarily under the pressure. However as always, hard work and determination saw her not only pass solidly but also to achieve both a Bachelor's and Master's degree! I have never doubted her capability even when she has had her own internal doubts.

I have witnessed Charlotte face several humongous hurdles and unimaginable pain. Through these hardships she has held her beautiful family together and continued to grow in strength. Through the tears my sister has emerged just as kind and beautiful but ever more determined.

Charlotte continues to inspire me today. Her story will undoubtedly touch everyone who reads this book in the same way she continues to inspire me. A wonderful mother of four, a gym enthusiast, church elder, and social butterfly, I look forward to witnessing her triumph over all challenges. Charlotte is the epitome of bold, courageous and steadfast. I can't wait to read her masterpiece.

Carole (Sister)

I met Charlotte over fifteen years ago. We first met through the national basketball club as our husbands were both members. I admire Charlotte's outer beauty which is matched by her intellect. She is down-to-earth, personable, and makes people feel welcome. Since I've known Charlotte she is a committed and hard-working individual who has always put her family first.

Charlotte has had a challenging traumatic past. By God's grace she has worked through her challenges and persevered with strength and courage.

In the last few years, I have seen Charlotte grow from strength to strength through her journey. She carries herself with courage to become the best version of herself.

Charlotte is an inspirational person and I believe we will all have something positive to take away from her story.

Love and light,

Daisy

Preface

Trauma to Transformed: Uncovering the Gems Within is a life-changing roadmap for those navigating the challenging terrain of trauma recovery. In this insightful and empowering book, readers are invited on a journey of self-discovery and healing, guided by the wisdom of author Charlotte Twycross (pseudonym used for privacy purposes).

Based on a true story, within these pages lies a captivating tale, blending fictional elements with real-life experiences to protect the identities of those involved. The author expertly blends these elements to embrace resilience, healing, and personal transformation.

Drawing from personal experience and professional expertise, Charlotte Twycross offers practical tools, compassionate insights, and actionable strategies to help you navigate the complexities of trauma and reclaim your inner strength.

Through the pages of *Uncovering the Gems Within*, you will explore the empowering gifts of strength, courage, and self-compassion as you embark on the path toward healing and wholeness. From unravelling the layers of past pain to embracing the beauty of their authentic selves, you will uncover the hidden treasures buried within their own hearts and minds.

With a blend of heartfelt storytelling, practical exercises, and empowering affirmations, *Uncovering the Gems Within* empowers readers to cultivate resilience, embrace vulnerability, and embark on a journey of self-discovery that leads to lasting transformation.

Whether you are navigating the aftermath of trauma or seeking to support someone on their healing journey, this book offers invaluable insights and guidance to illuminate the path from trauma to treasure.

In sharing my story, I offer reflections on lessons I've learned, along with prayer points, Scriptures, and songs that have inspired me. This ongoing process of reflection and growth helps me embrace the fullness of life's possibilities. As you reflect on your life's journey, I hope you will experience deep transformations as we walk this path together.

Introduction

This memoir offers a candid and unfiltered account of my early childhood, experiences of molestation, and journey toward healing.

At first glance, my life may seem ordinary. But beneath the surface lie layers of scars, each one evidence of pain endured and resilience gained. This book is for anyone who has faced adversity, offering heartfelt insights and unwavering hope that God steadfastly watches over us through every trial.

Join me on a journey through my intricately woven life, where every thread tells a story of determination, triumph, and self-discovery. Through countless adversities, I rose time and again, defying the odds.

How did I navigate the traumatic events that sought to ensnare me? What role did hope, love, and God's unwavering presence play in my transformation?

Today, as a confident woman and mother of four wonderful children, I exemplify the power of perseverance. Despite decades of deception, manipulation, abuse, and confusion, I have unearthed the essence of my being. Each scar tells a tale of growth, shaping me into who I am today. I am proud of my journey and the invaluable lessons I've learned.

I write to share the tools and insights that propelled me on my path of self-discovery. I hope this book will uplift and empower you, giving you a deeper understanding of yourself. Whatever trials you face, there is always hope, and you possess the strength to overcome them.

As you delve into my story, may it guide you through your journey. Remember, someone else's burden may be heavier. Many people struggle with various forms of trauma, but with the right tools and emotional management, it is possible to persevere and overcome.

It has taken me over four decades to reach this moment of clarity and self-acceptance. I cherish my children's love. Through this extreme journey, I have learned to embrace my true self and understand the intricate dimensions of my life's events.

Now I aim to use my voice to champion resilience, strength, and healing from trauma for women and children everywhere.

I invite you to apply the secrets in the final section to guide and nurture those in your sphere of influence to rise and win in their uniqueness and inner strength.

I pray this book will encourage you to believe that nothing is insurmountable with hope, faith, and self-respect.

Gratefully,

Charlotte Twycross

Today I Am Five [Poem]

Today I'm five
Today I'm alive
Life is beautiful
It's easy
I'm going to get ice cream
I'm going to get some sweets
I'm skipping in the sunshine soaking up the sun
It's beautiful
What am I going to have for lunch?
I can't wait.
I am awake
I'm happy
I'm joyful - life is so easy
I wonder what mum is making for dinner?
I wonder if I'll be allowed to stay up late and watch TV
Oh no!
I forgot my bag, oh dear!
Life is so easy
Life is so simple
I love being me
This child is Carefree
Happy
It's not complicated
It's simple
I love this moment
Today, I am five

Charlotte

Part One

While our destinies are set in motion from the moment we are born, sometimes they are hijacked by unexpected life events.

As we begin this eventful journey together, consider:

What childhood dreams have you manifested? What has been derailed?

As they say, life is not a bed of roses…

Chapter One: *Meet Charlotte*

The day of my birth was marked by rain-soaked skies, prompting my mother to proclaim, "*Showers of blessings are raining on me.*" Indeed, as I reflect on my life's journey, I am overwhelmed by the countless blessings that have graced my path. Despite the twists and turns, this is my story, my melody...

Mum's account of my birth

I worked till noon on the Saturday preceding your arrival. My sceptical boss wondered whether I was ready to deliver, expecting me to return to work the following Monday. As a precaution, I delegated my duties to a newcomer, acquainting her with file management and other essential tasks.

News of an impending solar eclipse stirred warnings not to gaze directly at it, to avoid jeopardizing the well-being of my unborn child. Taking heed, I retreated home, sealed all the windows and drew the curtains in the house shared with two Sudanese ladies while my husband toiled in another town.

Indoors, I meticulously arranged my surroundings, packed baby clothes, and anticipated an early arrival, as clinical staff had warned to expect. Exhausted, I retired early, steering clear of the eclipse's sight. However, early on Sunday morning, an unfamiliar tummy pain jolted me awake with a start. Since I'd had a painless pregnancy, I initially dismissed them as inconsequential.

Repeated trips to the restroom prompted concern from housemates, who urged me to seek medical attention, foreseeing an imminent birth.

The ladies said, *"If you won't let us take you to the clinic you may end up delivering in the house and it's your first baby."* Obligingly, they took me to the clinic. When we said we were going to the maternity ward, the taxi driver asked who was having a baby. Pointing at me, he declared confidently, *"Not you."* When I responded, *"Yes, it's me,"* he nearly collided with another car in disbelief.

Didn't I look 'ripe enough' to deliver so soon? The sceptical taxi driver must have thought not. Meanwhile, once we arrived at the hospital, the attending staff greeted us with astonishment after discovering how advanced my labour was.

Overwhelmed with joy, I welcomed my gorgeous daughter into the world at noon. Entranced by my baby's presence, despite the nurses' advice to rest, the thought of parting from her for even a few moments was agonising. When a brief attempt to tend to personal needs resulted in a stumble, thankfully, hospital staff were swift to intervene.

Back in bed, the gnawing hunger threatened to steal the blissful peace and calm. Since hospital protocol restricted outside food, staff phoned a family member for assistance. Before long, my body was refuelled after gratefully tucking into a nourishing meal prepared by a close relative.

After spending the night under observation, I returned home the following morning, where my sister-in-law nurtured me. Both grandmothers received the joyful news of your arrival. This marked the beginning of a beautiful time, filled with love, warmth, and family support.

Farm Life

My father's frequent travels defined my early years, leaving Mum as the primary caregiver. A contented baby, I basked in my family's affection and cherished moments with cousins. However, an aversion to darkness and a fear of spiders and creepy crawlies marked my childhood, alongside peculiar fascinations with the intricacies of ants' movements.

Waking up in our home, with a view overlooking the majesty of Table Mountain National Park in Cape Town, was a daily blessing that filled me with awe. The Cape Peninsula boasted other iconic landmarks such as Lion's Head, Signal Hill, and the Atlantic Ocean coastline, all contributing to the region's breathtaking scenery. The park, renowned for its magnificent landscapes and extensive network of hiking trails, was a great panoramic viewpoint of the city, coastline, and surrounding mountains.

My grandma's farm was behind our home, nestled within the National Park. I have fond memories of helping with chores like sweeping the yard and tending to the cows and goats housed in their mud-built shelter near the fireplace, where we slept.

Our daily routine often involved gathering firewood from the farm and carrying it home. I resembled an acrobat balancing heavy loads supported on a bright rolled-up African printed sheet on the head. Despite my slender frame, I discovered the inner strength to manage these burdens, even when trekking miles to fetch water from a distant well, all while balancing a large bucket over my head. Fortunately, I avoided mishaps like tumbling down the field or being chased by goats.

One of my cherished pastimes was climbing trees to retrieve ripened mangoes and bananas, adding a touch of adventure to my days. Bathing outdoors with a bucket and plastic cup was another exhilarating experience, though in hindsight, using the outdoor toilet (a massive manhole) seemed perilous.

I vividly recall a near-drowning incident while returning from delivering maize to the flour mill. Accidentally slipping on a muddy stream ledge, I found myself submerged and panic-stricken. Through sheer determination, I somehow managed to pull myself to safety by hanging on to the reeds. Since that day, an unhealthy fear of water has lingered. Unsurprisingly, even after four decades, mastering the art of swimming continues to elude me.

Unlike most children my age who start formal schooling at five years, mine didn't commence in South Africa. Hence, I missed out on attending nursery, kindergarten, and the typical introduction to using tools like pencils and paper. Nonetheless, I was fluent in Xhosa, our native language in Cape Town.

When my family relocated to France at the age of 7, my French vocabulary was limited to just two words: **Oui** meaning 'yes' and **Non** meaning 'no'. Imagine the confusion in conversations where I would often unintentionally respond affirmatively when I meant the opposite, much to the amusement of my listeners!

Education

Early memories of my childhood in France are quite vivid and filled with a sense of wonder. My heart bubbled over with excitement when we landed at Charles de Gaulle Airport, amazed and privileged to embark on a new chapter in a different continent. Our home in Villa Place,

Nantes, was nestled in a charming neighbourhood that provided a warm and welcoming environment for our family.

My time at École Sainte-Zoé in West Nantes was filled with fond memories and challenges. Being one of the few black children at the school, my classmates curiously approached me to touch my hair and skin, as if trying to understand or even change my appearance. At the time, I felt uniquely special and included. I naively thought this attention made me popular, but looking back, I realize it was a form of racism that I didn't fully grasp as a child.

My best friend, Lauren, provided comfort and support during those early days at school. Despite my limited French vocabulary, Lauren helped me navigate the language barrier and made me feel included.

Growing up in Nantes accorded opportunities to learn French and integrate into the community. Despite the challenges, I embraced school life, eagerly tackling homework assignments and immersing myself in every aspect of my education. Outside of school, I cherished moments spent with my siblings Carole and Hannah who brought joy and laughter into our home. School days were filled with adventure and discovery. The days were long but fulfilling as I walked to and from school.

Family dynamics played a significant role in shaping my childhood experiences. Mum's demanding work schedule meant I rarely saw her as she toiled tirelessly during the day and into the night, sometimes even on weekends.

Despite my young age, I took on significant responsibility and learned to cook and care for my younger siblings, gaining valuable life skills.

In contrast, my father, a diligent student on the path to becoming an Architect, was a constant presence in our lives. He fulfilled his parental duties and went above and beyond the call of duty, cooking and caring for us in ways that exceeded expectations.

Reflecting on those early years in France fills me with gratitude for my family's love, support and steadfastness that helped me overcome challenges and thrive in a new environment.

Early maturity and startling discovery

One morning, I awoke to a startling sight: a pool of blood surrounding me. Confused and frightened, I wondered if I was gravely ill, unaware that my menstruation had just begun. At eight years old, I was entirely ignorant of the change puberty brings to a girl's body. In those times, discussions about early adolescence were absent both at home and in school, leaving me bewildered by the natural progression from childhood to puberty.

Reflecting on my early menstruation at the age of eight, it's not surprising considering my poor diet at the time which lacked essential nutrients. As a child, I indulged in copious amounts of unhealthy foods, delighting in oily sausages and dipping bread into the grease, considering it a delicacy. In the winter months, I relished sucking out bone marrow immersed in hearty broth soups.

Concerned about my weight, the school summoned my parents to address my unhealthy lifestyle. Consequently, they began incorporating more vegetables into my diet. However, this dietary change didn't prevent the painful outbreaks between my thighs, which I attempted to alleviate with talcum powder, to no avail.

However, despite this dietary change, I continued to experience painful skin irritations and flare-ups between my thighs, likely caused by chafing and excessive friction.

Desperate attempts to soothe the discomfort with talcum powder failed miserably with hardly any relief. Acne plagued my back, face, and chest as the friction between my thighs escalated to painful blisters.

New Residence

When I turned ten, we bid farewell to the seaside town and ventured into the bustling city of Nantes. Our new abode was a snug three-bedroomed flat in town, brimming with fond memories shared with my parents before my siblings arrived.

From the lounge window in our Mink Gardens home, the spacious playing field below beckoned invitingly. Unfortunately, we were rarely allowed to venture beyond our four walls since mum and dad were apprehensive about our safety. Undeterred, we ingeniously devised games to while away the hours indoors.

One amusing pastime involved playing paper tennis. We fashioned balls from crumpled paper, set a row of books as a makeshift net and ladybird books as rackets. Occasionally we were permitted to watch television. Still, our hearts yearned to explore the nearby park where we could mingle with other children. Our spirited antics, like hastily pretending to be studying when our parents returned home, became a hallmark of our days.

Our rare family excursions involved strolls along the beach, followed by delectable picnic food. Once back home, boredom would often lead to mischievous antics with my siblings. We took turns to vigilantly watch for dad's return. By the time the key turned on the door, we'd be settled at the table, trying to appear engrossed in our studies. Interestingly, our escapades often ended with Hannah's capture and Carole shouldering blame; the reasons behind the scapegoating remained a mystery.

After our move, my daily journey to and from secondary school led me across the field. Though walking alone felt dangerous, the allure of the beautiful bandstand in the park often drew me in. There, I danced and crafted my own joy.

At school, I was fiercely competitive and exceptionally diligent. Nearly every Friday assembly, I found myself called onto the stage to receive a *'Certificat de Bonne Nouvelle'* ('Good News Certificate'). If it wasn't me, it was my close friend Freda. Our academic prowess propelled us to be promoted a grade higher, excelling particularly in Maths and English. Had scholarships been available in our day, we might have secured spots in prestigious private schools. Sadly, that honour didn't land on our laps.

When I turned fourteen I sat for my 'Brevet' (middle school) exams a year ahead of schedule, completing my 'Baccalauréat' Maths by fifteen. With a penchant for mathematics, I opted for a comprehensive array of Maths courses and glided through the exams.

Work Mindset

From a young age, we were taught the value of hard work and dedication, setting the foundation for a healthy work mindset that has guided me throughout my life. This invaluable lesson has propelled me forward, shaping my approach to achieving success.

One vivid memory that encapsulates this ethos is my frequent visits to the reference library, a sanctuary of knowledge where I spent countless hours immersed in research and further reading. To ensure I arrived promptly I caught the early bus eager to secure the prime seating area where I could delve into my studies undisturbed.

My passion for learning drove me to linger in the library long after others had departed, determined to complete my research thoroughly. This commitment to excellence and continuous improvement has been a cornerstone of my work ethic, driving me to strive for the best in all aspects of my life.

Consequences of Misbehaving

Carole most frequently experienced the repercussions of misbehaviour. She seemed to encounter the disciplinary measures, often in the form of a 'chastising tool' (a long bamboo stick used for smacking) more frequently than any of us. Her fiery and determined nature earned her the reputation of being a rebel among us.

Socializing was very limited. My parents had strict rules about interacting with school friends, prohibiting visits or invitations to our home. Being isolated meant that I missed out on the typical childhood joys of bonding and creating memorable moments with friends.

Within our close-knit circle of family friends, we visited each other for birthday parties, barbecues and dinner parties. Whenever we hosted, Dad was in his element; the ever-smiling, happy, generous host. If there was an award for this, he would have won it for sure. Even if we had nothing or very little he would empty all our pockets and savings to show everyone that he had plenty and give the illusion that we were not really struggling financially.

New Sibling's Arrival

Nana Stella came to live with us when Mum was expecting Tracey, filling our home with excitement about our baby sister's imminent arrival. As my confirmation approached, the Vicar conducted our lessons at his home, a setup that seemed to displease Dad. The confirmation ceremony was at our local church shortly after my 14th birthday.

Not long after, we celebrated Carole's tenth birthday with a delightful ginger cake Mum baked. Carole also received an amazing birthday airplane from Uncle Dan, the aviation enthusiast.

Nana eagerly observed the differences between her homeland and her new surroundings. In summertime, she was surprised by how lightly everyone dressed in sharp contrast to back home. Realizing it was due to the limited sunshine they enjoyed, Nana eventually adapted and grew to enjoy it. She was also intrigued by the variety of television shows available.

Chatting with her grandchildren, exchanging stories, and comparing life back home to France were cherished moments. Shopping trips thrilled her with their abundance, despite the shocking prices. Overall, their time together was filled with laughter and precious memories.

Sometime later, Nana grew homesick although she enjoyed spending quality time with us. With heavy hearts, we bid her farewell as she boarded the flight home, leaving behind fond memories.

Food poisoning: Christmas Aftermath

One Christmas, we eagerly feasted on a beautifully roasted turkey, confident in its perfection. Unexpectedly, within a few hours, struck by food poisoning and writhing in pain, we made frantic trips to the restroom. The doctor identified the culprit: the turkey hadn't fully thawed, leaving the interior undercooked. This harsh lesson cast a shadow over our holiday celebration.

Vital lesson: Always seek expert advice on how to prepare new recipes.

Discovering Nantes' Blissful Delights

As the vibrant sun rose over the charming city of Nantes, France, anticipation filled the air as I embarked on an adventure to the local street market and jumble sales. With a skip in my step and a twinkle in my eye, I set off through the bustling streets, eager to explore the treasures that awaited me.

Arriving at the market, I was greeted by a kaleidoscope of colours and sounds. The aroma of freshly baked bread mingled with the sweet scent of flowers, while the chatter of vendors and shoppers filled the air with energy and excitement. With each step, I discovered a new delight, from vibrant fruits and vegetables to handcrafted artisan goods.

The jumble sales captured my vivid imagination. Rows of tables overflowing with trinkets and treasures beckoned to me, promising hidden gems waiting to be uncovered. With a sense of exhilaration, I dove into the sea of merchandise, my eyes gleaming with anticipation as I sifted through the eclectic mix of items.

Within the chaos, I stumbled upon a stall selling delicacy marrow bones, a local specialty that piqued my curiosity. With a sense of adventure coursing through my veins, I eagerly purchased a bone, eager to relive the delicious experience.

Finding a quiet spot amidst the market's hustle and bustle, I settled in to savour the bones. With each succulent bite, I was transported to food heaven, the rich, velvety texture melting in my mouth and tantalizing my taste buds with its savoury goodness. It was a tasty experience like no other, a true taste of Nantes's culinary prowess.

After indulging in the market's delightful bites, I made my way to an English-speaking church in Nantes, seeking solace and community in a foreign land. On entering the church, I was greeted by the warm embrace of fellow worshippers, their voices raised in joyful praise.

Surrounded by the comforting familiarity of English speakers, I found a sense of belonging and connection in this foreign land. Together, we shared in the spirit of fellowship and worship, united by our common faith and shared experiences.

As I left the church, my heart was full, my senses alive with the sights, sounds, and flavours of Nantes. It had been a day of adventure and discovery, affirming the beauty and richness of life in this amazing city. As I made my way home, I carried with me memories that would last a lifetime, cherishing every miracle that awaited me at every corner in Nantes.

Time to reflect

List 3 things that made your childhood happy and memorable. Why are these moments so important to you today?

Did you feel heard and cherished as a child? What did you do when things didn't go according to plan?

In hindsight, is there anything you would have done differently given a second chance at being a child?

Share some examples.

Chapter Two: *Twisted Teens*

On May 1st, I officially stepped into my teenage years, though the day didn't hold any particularly memorable moments. I wasn't the epitome of a typical teenager; instead, I grappled with various physical discomforts, including back acne, blotchy spots, and severe acne on my face. As a voluptuous teen with rounded curves, I often endured the discomfort of my thighs rubbing together, especially exacerbated by the sweltering summer heat.

As fashion wasn't my priority, I often scoured various sale spots in more affluent areas. Despite our modest means, charity shops offered an opportunity to enhance our wardrobes affordably, allowing us to find some amazing outfits for just a few Francs (before the currency switched to Euros).

My childhood lacked the typical celebrations or indulgences like birthday cakes or outings to McDonald's or KFC, which made me feel disconnected from others. Without a conventional childhood, growing up marred by grooming and unhappiness left me with less-than-ideal memories of my teens.

To make matters worse, fear permeated much of my adolescence as I grappled with unsettling feelings and uncertainties.

With no outlet for my emotions, I internalized my fears and soldiered on, hoping for a day when truth would bring liberation—an eventual reality detailed further in this book.

My first excursion away from home occurred during my best friend's father's funeral. Despite being immersed in various emotions I was somehow able to provide support and empathy for my friend during her time of need.

The strict monitoring and disciplinary measures faced at home shaped me significantly, instilling a sense of structure and methodical approach to tasks. These traits continue to define my character today.

Manipulated Innocence

As I stepped into the threshold of early adulthood at the age of eighteen, I found myself carrying the weight of a lifetime's worth of challenges, each experience etching its mark on my existence. From the innocent days of childhood to the tumultuous storms of adolescence, I had walked a path filled with obstacles and trials, each one shaping me in ways I had yet to fully comprehend.

An unwelcome secret, heavy as a stone, silently weighed me down. Unprepared to endure the unexpected, unwanted pregnancy from my dad, termination was the only alternative. Each step taken in secrecy was fraught with pain and solitude, locking away the turmoil and anguish within the crevices of my aching soul. I built a fortress around my memories, shielding myself from the raw emotions that threatened to overwhelm me.

Discarding the key to my inner sanctuary, I hoped to bury the painful past and focus solely on the present moment to survive.

In retrospect, I see the limitations of this coping mechanism, the cracks in my armour becoming increasingly apparent with every passing day. Yet, in the absence of guidance and support from trusted adults, I was adrift in a sea of uncertainty, navigating the treacherous waters of young adulthood with little more than sheer determination to guide me.

Through the fog of forgetfulness, one memory stands out with chilling clarity—a nightmarish tableau of my father's twisted ritual, a grotesque display of control and dominance that left me feeling powerless and vulnerable. With bloodied wrists and threats of violence hanging in the air like a dark cloud, he wielded his power like a weapon, leaving me paralyzed with fear and uncertainty.

My journey to adulthood was a turbulent voyage through the depths of despair, a relentless struggle against the forces that sought to break me. Bereft of the semblance of a normal childhood, I was thrust into a world of pain and suffering, the scars of which would linger long after the physical wounds had healed. And yet, amidst the darkness, there remained a glimmer of hope—a small spark of resilience that refused to be extinguished, a light in the shadows that whispered the promise of redemption and renewal yet to come. Pause and take a moment to reflect on your own journey.

Time to reflect

In what ways have some of your teen memories reflected how you were raised in your early years?

Were there certain people you may have talked to about your confusion who might have helped to build your coping mechanisms in your teenage years (example: parent, relative, close friend, other)?

What strategies did you apply to guide your emotional healing?

Chapter Three: *Ripple Effect of my Parents' Lifestyles*

I interviewed Mum to gain a deeper understanding of her experiences, motivations and how they have impacted our lives.

Mum's upbringing

Mum's upbringing within her family was nothing short of idyllic, a dream that felt like the standard every family should aspire to. With loving and attentive parents who fostered an atmosphere of freedom and support, Mum felt very blessed. Growing up as the eldest among five siblings, they all enjoyed a carefree existence under their parents' nurturing guidance, a lifestyle she hoped to replicate in her own adulthood.

Even as young adults, the siblings maintained close ties, returning home for significant events or to offer support during times of illness. However, as each sibling embarked on their own journey through marriage and life's challenges, their interactions inevitably transitioned to occasional contacts, yet remained meaningful.

Throughout it all, Mum and her siblings found guidance in their parents' unwavering support and wisdom. The daily prayers for their marriages and families provided strength and reassurance.

Understanding my parents' daily routines and motivations helped me appreciate their struggles and uncover the gaps that inevitably influenced the person I am today.

Childhood Kindness

You were always friendly and kind, even with your younger siblings, who adored you. At just six years old, you eagerly helped, feeding your sister without hesitation whenever I needed to rush out. You were so lovely and sweet.

Teenage Years

As a teenager, you looked forward to going out, but your social interactions were limited to school. Joanne and Maria were your best friends, but your friendship was confined to school hours. At home, your primary focus was homework. You always went everywhere with your family under strict supervision, which prevented you from enjoying the typical teenage freedoms. Even at school, you were closely monitored, making it difficult for you to have a normal teenage experience.

Mum's Responsibilities

As a nurse, Mum worked long shifts and was often not home. After exhausting hours in hospices or hospitals, she needed to catch up on sleep during the day. On her days off, she would bake bread and cook with us. Mum was dedicated to her work and providing for the family. Her job required long hours, travel on public transport, and a constant rush to prepare meals before heading off to her next shift, often far away. Running to catch the train was a regular part of her day.

When Mum returned from her late night shifts we were already asleep, our homework done. She would then wash up and go straight to bed and repeat the cycle the next day. Saturdays meant working in the morning and then spending the weekend catching up on all the tasks that had piled up during the week. This demanding routine continued throughout our teenage years, with Dad taking care of us in Mum's absence.

Social life

Mum's social circle was limited to two family friends who occasionally visited our home. She refrained from venturing out and viewed her acquaintances as superficial, unable to confide in them about personal matters. The sole common ground they shared was their roles as mothers.

Interactions primarily revolved around discussions about children—celebrating their accomplishments and addressing any challenges they faced. However, Mum ceased confiding in these women after realizing they were merely using her to gather information. In the end, she found solace and genuine companionship only among her own relatives.

Impact of First-born syndrome

Initially, as the eldest in my family my parents set high expectations and doted on me. Subconsciously, I naturally assumed the trailblazer role for my siblings as the first to experience everything from puberty trials to school challenges. Driven by a sense of responsibility, I worked tirelessly to set a positive example for my younger siblings and constantly aimed to meet my parents' expectations, hoping to make them proud.

My younger siblings, Hannah, Carole, and Tracey looked to me for guidance. The invaluable lessons from my late grandmother's nurturing care and wisdom and Mum's love continually hold a special place in my heart. I am grateful for the solid foundation they provided during my formative years.

Mum's amazing cooking and hospitality filled our home with warmth, and occasional gatherings with extended family brought joy. Yet, despite these moments of merriment, strict rules often barred us from attending school friends' birthday parties, contrasting with the exhilaration of our first family movie outing.

Special Heartfelt Message

Do you love receiving unexpected special messages from your nearest and dearest? Here's the heart-warming message my children sent me:

Good morning mummy,

I love you. Happy Mother's Day.

God blessed me with the best mother a daughter could ask for and I thank God for you every day.

You raised me to be the person I am today and I am eternally grateful for everything you have done for me..

We all love and appreciate you always although we may not always show it.

We hope you have the best Mother's Day.

You deserve the world! 🩶 🌐

Love from my children.

Time to reflect

Did you have a joyful childhood and family life?

How were your relationships and interactions with family members?

How did you address challenges as a family?

What would you do differently now as an adult? If you have your own family, what would you emulate? What would you avoid?

Chapter Four: *Two-Faced Parenting*

Not all that glitters is gold.

Dad's violent streak

Dad had peculiar habits, one of which involved touching the television to gauge its temperature. Strangely, he forbade us from watching it in his absence, punishing us severely if we dared to disobey.

In his foul moods, or when provoked by our careless remarks, Dad would suddenly reach for the dreaded wooden spoon and administer harsh punishment that left us feeling both intimidated and fearful.

A particularly harrowing incident remains etched in Hannah's memory. While washing dishes, Carole inadvertently drew Dad's wrath with a simple response. Enraged, he lashed out with the wooden spoon, striking Carole relentlessly. Shocked and furious, Hannah and I quickly intervened, shielding our sister from further harm, refusing to condone Dad's violent actions any longer.

Coping with covert family struggles

Children often fail to grasp the hidden complexities that strain their parents' relationships, and we were no exception. Strange occurrences and interactions at home left me confused. Any questions my siblings and I asked about our parents' relationship were met with silence and strategic ignorance.

Mum was emotionally traumatised and in denial. Her significant absence during my crucial formative years deepened my confusion and sense of abandonment, leaving many questions unanswered. Growing up with constantly fighting parents can leave deep emotional scars, especially when one is known and respected in the community.

My father relished displaying his status and wealth. To outsiders, he appeared successful and admirable, leading many to call me a *daddy's girl*. However, this label could not have been further from the truth. Beneath his polished exterior, my father was a psychopathic high achiever who cared only about himself. His charm masked a deeply selfish nature, where poor moral choices were made without fear of consequences or consideration for others. In his world, sin was the norm.

His public persona sharply contrasted with his private behaviour. While he basked in the adulation of our community, his true character emerged behind closed doors. The staff who worked for him saw a different side, often describing him as a mean and angry person.

This environment was particularly challenging for me as I navigated the dichotomy of public perception and private reality. The constant tension and hostility at home were inescapable, resulting in significant emotional turmoil.

Living in such a volatile atmosphere affected every aspect of my life. The fights between my parents were not just verbal but emotional battles that left me feeling helpless and insecure. The facade of a perfect family was maintained for appearances, but the cracks were evident to anyone who looked closely. My father's relentless need to project an image of success and control only exacerbated the trauma, as it became clear that his love and attention were conditional and superficial.

These experiences have had a long-lasting impact, shaping my understanding of relationships and trust, often making it difficult to form healthy connections with others. The pain of witnessing my father's callous disregard for anyone's well-being but his own has left a lingering sense of betrayal and disillusionment. Even as I strive to move beyond these memories, the lessons learned in that tumultuous setting continue to influence my perspectives and choices.

Reflecting on these challenges, I recognize the importance of breaking the cycle of dysfunction. Understanding the roots of my trauma is a crucial step towards healing and ensuring I do not perpetuate the same patterns in my own life. By acknowledging the truth behind the facade, I aim to foster an environment of honesty and compassion, where genuine connections can flourish free from the shadows of past pain.

Time to reflect

Did you experience doubts or confusion about the relationships between the adults who surrounded you as a child?

How did that impact your life as a teenager and into adulthood? (Reflect on family relationships and other friendships in terms of communication, confidence, trust and more).

Chapter Five: *Supporting Children Through Challenges*

Navigating manipulation, abusive relationships, and betrayal from close family members constitutes the deepest form of agony any child can endure. I am deeply grateful for God's enduring grace, love, and healing power without which my existence would hold little value.

Anger manifests in various forms, often stemming from the inability to articulate one's pain. It may manifest as sadness, internalized rage, or mistreatment of others. Such behaviours frequently mask unspoken suffering caused by feelings of neglect, rejection, or being unheard.

My journey involved channelling this energy through prayer, seeking support from loved ones, engaging in physical and mental exercises, and finding solace in literature and cinema.

Decisions for Children

Children sometimes notice anomalies in the home and start to question them. Consider the following dilemmas.

A wedding ring is symbolic. When a spouse suddenly stops wearing it, children will notice it and wonder what may have happened between mum and dad.

Other areas of concern include sleeping habits and locations between couples. For example, wondering why daddy sleeps in the front room where previously he shared the bedroom with mummy.

Younger children may frame their concerns differently, for example:

Why is daddy not here?

Why doesn't daddy speak to me?

Why are we not a family?

Why can't daddy come back home and find work near us so he can live with us?

Why don't we have a bigger car like before?

Why does mummy have to travel on the bus with us while daddy drives the car to work?

These questions all demonstrate the youngsters' varied conflicting emotions. They are also signs of sadness and confusion as children seek their parents' physical presence in their lives. Children need to be nurtured and loved tangibly while both parents play a pivotal role in ensuring the child's overall wellbeing and confidence.

Lack of physical touch, presence, empathy, support, and nurturing leaves a void that can result in a child becoming introverted and hiding deep wounds. If these questions are not addressed the emotional trauma may create deeper challenges in adulthood.

Time to reflect

Are you a parent? Yes / No

Within your family, how might your behaviour and actions before your healing affect your children's behaviour and feelings?

Not understanding who we really are creates an emotional disconnect for parents raising their own families. Did you or someone you know experience any coping dilemmas? What strategies were applied?

Which of these would you consider: *counselling, talking therapy, speaking to a religious leader, trusted adult, health professional* (General Practitioner, nurse), *teacher or adult*? (Circle all that apply)

Name some ways you would have sought for help with the major issues you faced as a teenager.

Part Two

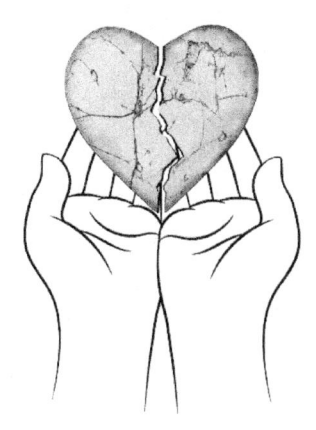

The journey toward emotional healing intricately intertwined with my spiritual growth and created a deeper faith in God. Although I cannot detail every lesson learned during this season, prayer, introspection, and the influence of positive role models emerged as central themes throughout.

The period of healing highlighted the importance of seeking solace in prayer which allowed me to connect with God and find strength in His presence. Reflective practices helped me gain insights into my experiences and navigate through moments of difficulty with greater clarity and understanding.

Additionally, the impact of uplifting role models provided guidance and encouragement, shaping my perspective and inspiring me to persevere on my journey of healing and spiritual maturation.

Chapter Six: *Trauma Triggers*

Desperate for emotional and spiritual growth, I attended talking therapies at a nearby medical facility and was encouraged to create time for spiritual development.

Identifying Trauma Triggers

To a fourteen-year-old teen, the adult is physically bigger and stronger. The child can't stop the adult from taking advantage because they feel powerless, vulnerable, caged and trapped with no way out. When the male attacker advances the child feels insignificant and suffocated by the antagonist's size and power. My therapist suggested I continued with the healing therapy, noting this was a lifelong journey.

While many parents may advise the child to 'tell an adult', this is not straightforward for several reasons.

Why a child may not tell

They may have been threatened with severe punishment, physical harm or manipulated into giving in to intimate advances against the child's will. A young girl may fear for her life if she stops doing everything he wants her to.

She may not tell an adult due to fear of the threats and consequences. Furthermore, she may have no trustworthy friends or adults to tell. When the female parent is never there, the child is not as close to the mother they are to the father which creates a parenting imbalance.

Children need and crave for physical comfort of both parents to nurture them. A daughter who is close to the father may trust and allow him to do things or touch them in ways they instinctively sense to be inappropriate.

Sometimes, the antagonist may take it a step further and add emotional and spiritual manipulation. For example, my abuser used a gruesome form of blackmail which involved a blood ritual where he cut my wrist and drew blood from his own wrist, joining our wrists, stating this was our top secret. I could never tell anyone if I wanted my siblings and me to live.

His strategic manipulation included making comments about my weight and appearance which made me feel vulnerable, powerless. My confidence was systematically stripped to the point where I felt I had no say in the matter. Always wanting to please him, I obliged, all the while wondering what would happen if I chose to tell someone. But who could I tell? Mum was always out working; without any close aunt to confide in, I felt stuck.

Decades later, I still have no answers for why dad wanted to abuse me; I would sure love to find out!!

Abuser's justification

He claimed that children needed to be educated early about the 'facts of life' to avoid any unwanted pregnancy. Yet this did not stop him impregnating me in my teens!

Impediments to sound judgments

Alcohol which lowers intuition and causes antagonists to do things they would not normally do when sober. This was always the excuse used whenever I enquired!

Excuses given for the abuse:

I was well developed, pretty, the eldest daughter, quiet (therefore less likely to tell on him). I trustingly cuddled the abuser, sat on his knee and enjoyed the attention.

During our counselling sessions we unpicked each of these excuses. This was crucial to help me understand the gravity of the systematic manipulation, misinformation and lies my abuser had repeatedly used to brainwash my mind.

Well developed.

He should have controlled his urges and fantasies. You are a child, and he should never have laid a finger on you.

Pretty

He should not have looked at you in that way or done any of those things because of how you looked.

The eldest

He should not have inflicted abuse on you because you are the eldest or used it to set an example for your siblings. That is wrong.

Quiet

He used your innocence, trust, and developing body and emotions; it was wrong.

Too loving

That is no excuse to take advantage of you and abuse you.

Cuddling the abuser

All children like to be cuddled. It does not mean he had the right to take this further and abuse you.

Sat on knee

Children enjoy sitting on their parents' laps for comfort. It does not mean this gives them the right to touch and abuse you.

Enjoyed the attention and wrongly equated it with love

Children should enjoy their parents' attention which is often a form of parental love. Taking it further was wrong.

Time to Reflect

Do you know anyone who has experienced confusion and trauma from unexplained actions from someone they loved and trusted?

Briefly explain what happened.

What encouragement would you give them to support their healing from what you have discovered in this chapter?

Chapter Seven: *The Healing Journey*

TAKE CARE OF YOUR MIND

Creating time for daily Bible reading was essential. God has an amazing way of turning our weaknesses into strength when we yield to His love, power and guidance.

Forgive.

The first faith step towards my healing journey was finding the heart to forgive. Forgiveness reduces layers of resentment. It is important to apply the Holy Spirit's power to everything that needs to be forgiven.

Since forgiveness is not easy, spiritual mentorship was necessary. The *Alpha Course* was a game changer. I had a series of fifteen 90-minute sessions which helped to realign my mind with the truth of God's Word concerning me.

To help normalise life I attended a counselling session with a lovely lady who encouraged me to read a certain book and complete the exercises focused on *enriching yourself*.

Focus: *What do I want?*

Emotional development

Unfortunately, my childhood traumas carried on through to adulthood since they were not addressed. It is important to note that the abused has no say in the relationship. An unequal power distribution results in manipulation, coercion, and low self-esteem. My unstable childhood led to stifled growth into adulthood mentally and emotionally.

Separation from the home environment to attend boarding school as a child created a rift with my parents. Forced to grow up prematurely, I constantly yearned for my mother as I was not independent enough to look after myself amongst strangers. At the boarding school, I felt very vulnerable and often broke down. My confidence shattered, I felt like it didn't matter and found it hard to trust others.

As I grew into adulthood, there was a constant feeling of danger lurking nearby. My relationship with my husband was unequal; he hardly participated in nurturing the relationship. He found it easier to manipulate and punish me rather than treat me with respect and honour. In the end I sought my physical needs elsewhere.

Note: *Affairs get something that's missing including closeness, interaction, intimacy, physical touch, being heard and listened to.*

The six sessions addressed marriage, abuse and children. In the process we uncovered different aspects of childhood tied to a range of age groups.

Writing to Release Childhood Trauma

During my therapeutic work, I discovered a powerful tool: writing. This gift offers numerous benefits, including clarity, self-expression, emotional relief, cognitive restructuring, empowerment, closure, stress reduction, memory consolidation, reframing, personal reflection, and improved communication. Writing is a valuable tool for personal healing and growth.

Writing about my traumatic experiences enabled me to process my emotions, release pent-up feelings, and alleviate emotional pain. Putting thoughts on paper helped me organize and make sense of overwhelming emotions.

Cognitive Benefits

Articulating my experiences helped consolidate and integrate fragmented memories, making them more coherent. Reframing these experiences, with the support of my mentor, provided new insights and perspectives.

Psychological Healing

Psychological healing is now evident in my life. Writing my story has enhanced my self-awareness and personal growth. Regularly writing about trauma is known to reduce symptoms of anxiety, depression, and PTSD. The reduction in stress has also provided an outlet for negative emotions and eased the burden of suppressing painful memories.

Physiological Benefits

Reduced stress through writing has positively impacted my physical health, including improved immune function and lower blood pressure.

Empowerment and Growth

Embracing personal empowerment, control, and self-worth was a key goal. I am grateful for the person I am becoming as I shape my story and reclaim my sense of worth. The sense of closure has helped me move forward and leave the past behind. My relationships have also improved as I can articulate my feelings and experiences more effectively. Writing has provided a creative outlet for expressing emotions and life events that may be difficult to convey otherwise.

Exploring my identity and self-expression through writing has strengthened my sense of self. Over time, writing has enabled me to track my emotional and psychological progress, serving as a valuable measure of how I've overcome challenges. By creating a private space for personal reflection, writing has allowed me to continually explore and understand my thoughts and feelings.

It was crucial for me to write about my feelings and recollections of the traumatic events I experienced as a child at the hands of a close relative.

Letter to my Abuser

You are a disgusting piece of filth. You ruined me, took my virginity, childhood, and everything from me. How dare you! You are a very sick man. You made me think it was right to drink alcohol and be promiscuous and do all those nasty acts you taught me. To make matters worse, I even enjoyed it. I hate you for abusing and removing my childhood innocence.

I have suffered throughout my life because of you. How I wish you were not in my life after all you have done to my sisters and me. You betrayed our trust as the head of the family. You are a nasty, selfish piece of scum. I hate you so much!!!

I became addicted getting pleasure wherever I can get it. You took advantage of me and made me pregnant, and you even wanted me to have the baby for you as you thought I would have a boy! I said no way. You are a sick man!

My marriage is ruined because of you. You damaged my mind and my physical needs, and I thank God for helping me survive this. But for Tracey, I would not be where I am today. I will not let what you did to me have any effect on my children, myself, or my marriage. I give back to you all the trust, pain, and anger.

You taught and showed me things I was not meant to have known at that age. You frightened me. You gave me alcohol, threatened and forced me to keep silent, and performed a blood ritual to shut me up. I was afraid and did not tell anyone.

You stalked me and did not allow me to have any friends, go out, or do anything. You controlled me. Any money I earned you took from me. You made me feel worthless and 'rewarded me' with the abuse which I was forced to endure.

You raped me and took away my virginity when I was only thirteen years old. Three decades later I am only receiving therapy.

Charlotte.

After penning my thoughts and recollections, I felt an immense sense of relief and liberation. The act of writing provided a cathartic release, allowing me to unburden myself of the heavy emotional weight I had carried for so long. It was as if a dam had burst, and all the suppressed emotions—anger, sadness, confusion, and fear—flowed out onto the paper, helping me reflect on my experiences.

The process also brought a sense of clarity and understanding. Articulating my feelings and memories helped me make sense of the chaos that had long resided within. Patterns and connections I hadn't noticed before became visible with greater self-awareness and understanding of how these experiences had shaped me.

Moreover, I felt empowered and in control of my narrative. Writing allowed me to reclaim my story, transforming it from a series of painful memories into a coherent narrative I could own and reflect upon. This sense of ownership over my past was incredibly empowering, as it enabled me to see myself not just as a victim, but as a survivor with the strength to confront and overcome trials.

Overall, writing about my traumas fostered a sense of healing and closure. This was a crucial step in my journey toward emotional recovery, helping me to process my past and move forward with renewed peace and hope.

Time to Reflect

Have you used writing as a way of expressing your thoughts?

In what ways has writing helped you grow in confidence and communicate with yourself and others?

Chapter Eight: *Reclaim Your Power and Self-Esteem*

PATIENCE *with my* **GROWTH**

My journey through writing and reflecting on my traumatic experiences has not only been a path to personal healing but also a beacon of hope and guidance for others. Here's how my experiences can help you and others reclaim your power, worth, and self-esteem:

Writing as a Tool for Empowerment

By sharing how writing helped me process my emotions and make sense of my experiences, I hope to inspire you to pick up a pen and start your own journey. Writing provides a safe, private space where you can express your deepest thoughts and feelings without judgment. It can be incredibly empowering to see your experiences laid out in front of you, to recognize your strength and resilience, and to start viewing yourself not just as a victim, but as a survivor with a story of prevailing through challenges.

Reclaiming Your Narrative

When you write about your past, you take control of your narrative. You become the author of your own story, which is a powerful act of reclaiming your identity and self-worth.

It allows you to consider how far you've come and the obstacles you've overcome, reinforcing your sense of self and boosting your self-esteem.

Forgiveness

Forgiveness is a key component of healing. It doesn't mean forgetting or excusing the harm done to you, but rather releasing the hold that these negative experiences have on your present life. Through writing, I found a way to forgive those who hurt me, which freed me from the burden of resentment and anger. This act of forgiveness can help you find peace and move forward with a lighter heart.

Acceptance

Acceptance is about acknowledging your past and its impact on you without letting it define your future. Writing helped me accept my experiences and integrate them into my life story. This acceptance allows you to understand that while your past shapes you, it doesn't determine your future. Embracing this mindset can lead to a healthier, more positive self-image.

Empathy

Writing fosters empathy, both for yourself and for others. By exploring your own pain and struggles, you develop a deeper understanding of and compassion for yourself. This empathy extends outward, helping you connect with others who have had similar experiences. Sharing your story can inspire others, showing them that they are not alone, and that healing is possible.

Release

Writing acts as a release valve for pent-up emotions. It's a way to let go of the negative emotions that have been weighing you down. This release is crucial for mental and emotional health, allowing you to make space for positive feelings and experiences. By releasing the past, you can start focusing on building a brighter future.

Focusing on a Brighter Future

Ultimately, writing is a tool for transformation. It helps you move from a place of pain and trauma to a place of hope and possibility. By documenting your journey, you can set goals, envision a positive future, and take proactive steps toward achieving it. Writing helps you maintain focus on your aspirations and dreams, providing a roadmap to a more fulfilling life.

Conclusion

My experiences with writing as a means of healing from childhood trauma have shown me that it's possible to reclaim your power, worth, and self-esteem. By embracing forgiveness, acceptance, empathy, and release, you can begin to focus on a brighter future.

I encourage you to start writing, to explore your own story, and to use this powerful tool to embark on your journey toward healing and self-discovery. Your past does not define you; your strength and persistence do. Together, we can transform our pain into a source of empowerment and inspiration for ourselves and others.

Time to reflect

What lifechanging event has helped to shape who you are today?

How can you use your experiences to empower others to reclaim their worth and self-esteem?

What are some phrases you will use to pen your empowering narrative?

Light from Light

Light from light, gift to gift, we lift;

We hold high, we praise, and grace with joy.

The light within shines bright, a radiant gift,

Its glow entices, revelling in bliss.

The good, the brilliant, the wonderful—all aglow,

From light to light, from gift to gift, we flow.

We explore, we give, and together we shine,

Making moves that encourage, embrace, align.

Reaching out, we gather, hearts entwined,

Faces smiling, in giving, joy we find.

Speaking life, connecting soul to soul,

In unity, we flourish, we are whole.

Forward we journey into the light of lights,

Gifts upon gifts, our collective heights.

With love and grace as our steadfast guide,

We bask in the glow, standing side by side.

Poem by Charlotte Twycross

Part Three

No man is an island. Everyone needs someone to uplift them and help them see the forest for the trees.

Learn how unexpected encounters led to my inner and physical healing.

I pray that through divine intervention, someone will see your gifts and call out the greatness within.

Chapter Nine: *Destiny Helpers*

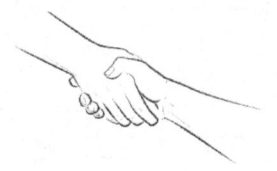

Divine helper #1:

Scarlet was the first person I met in France. As the 'angel' God brought into my life, she encouraged me to seek immediate medical help for a massive lump on my neck. Her Divine appointment and intervention helped to ensure I got the urgent surgery to restore my health. I'm forever grateful for God's intervention through Scarlet.

Divine helper #2:

In my mid 40s I started having extreme periods which included blood clots. Doctors suggested a hysterectomy or specific pill. I had a sense of urgency to get the surgery done quickly. 2 weeks later, the doctor said it was a miracle that the hidden cancerous fibroid, 3mm wide, was discovered and removed before it popped and spread into my internal organs. Praise the LORD, I've been cancer-free since.

Navigating illnesses and lessons learned

Much of my health struggles stem from decades of carrying deep-seated pain. Pretending that everything was fine, I would often don a mask of makeup. Like many others, I learned to conceal my inner turmoil behind a curtain of outward composure and forced smiles.

Enduring pain in silence was ingrained from a young age. We were taught to suppress suffering to avoid cultural stigma and familial disapproval. Our elders taught us to maintain a mask of submission and unquestioning obedience, especially within marriage, to preserve its sanctity at all costs.

However, this silence comes at a great cost to women's inner peace and fulfilment. When one's pain goes unheard and unseen, they become spiritually, physically, emotionally, and mentally damaged. Whether it's a learned behaviour by the oppressor or a deliberate act of disregard, being taken for granted leads to feelings of invisibility and worthlessness.

In such an environment, a woman's voice is neither welcomed nor acknowledged, stifling her ability to express her thoughts, feelings, and wisdom. This suppression of self-expression erodes her confidence and self-worth, creating a ripple effect that impacts her relationships and mental well-being.

Children raised in such environments witness their parents' devaluation and suppression, leading to confusion and emotional turmoil. They learn to mimic these behaviours, thereby perpetuating a cycle of dysfunction and fractured relationships.

The pressure to maintain appearances and keep up with societal expectations takes a toll on a woman's mental and physical health. Hypertension, anxiety, and suicidal thoughts often manifest resulting from prolonged stress and emotional suppression.

In the absence of healthy coping mechanisms, even minor changes can shatter a woman's fragile emotional state. Despite grappling with suicidal thoughts, something within me prevented me from succumbing to them, which served as a beacon of hope amidst the darkness.

The journey to where I stand today has been nothing short of miraculous, testifying to God's divine intervention. Throughout my life, from childhood to the present, I have felt God's guiding hand shaping my path, even during pain and uncertainty.

In my journey of healing and growth, I have been blessed with invaluable tools and support systems. From the unwavering love of family and friends to the guidance of mentors and counsellors, each person and resource has played a vital role in helping me navigate the complexities of trauma and find a path to healing and thriving.

But beyond the tangible tools and people, my faith and spiritual connection to God have been the cornerstone of my transformation. Through the trials and tribulations, I have drawn strength from the belief that God has a plan for me, guiding me towards a purposeful and fulfilling life.

Today, as I stand in the fullness of my being, I am filled with gratitude for the blessings that surround me. I share God's guiding light of love as my children's role model. My experiences have shaped me into a compassionate and thoughtful individual, driven by a passion to make a difference in the world.

Looking ahead, I am committed to using my voice to advocate for women and children everywhere. I am dedicated to breaking the silence surrounding trauma and promoting the importance of education and empowerment. Whether through setting up NGOs in remote villages, sharing my testimony with groups of women, or speaking on talk shows, I am determined to be a catalyst for positive change.

Working on this book with my publishing coach, Dr Jane Ellis, reminded me of the importance of nurturing open communication and shared desires within my own family. I am dedicated to creating beautiful memories with my children, ensuring they grow up knowing the depth of my love and dedication to them.

In the end, my journey from trauma to healing and thriving testifies to the power of faith, resilience, and the unwavering support of those around me. With God by my side and a commitment to making a difference, I am confident that my story will inspire and uplift others on their journey to healing and wholeness.

Time to reflect

What's your genius zone?

How have you honed your gifts and improved your skills?

How has sharing your skills empowered others?

Name 2-3 areas where you have grown in confidence and resilience.

Chapter Ten: *Growth And Development*

Life happens. Through mistakes we learn to embrace what is right.

Reflecting on my journey of healing and growth, I've come to recognize the importance of investing in myself and prioritizing my well-being. This journey has been marked by transformative experiences and valuable lessons, including:

Investing in Self-Worth and Spiritual Growth: Recognizing the inherent value within myself, I've embarked on a journey of self-discovery and spiritual nourishment. Through prayer, meditation, and introspection, I've cultivated a deeper sense of self-worth and embraced the path of spiritual growth.

Embracing Physical Fitness: Taking proactive steps towards physical health, I've embraced the challenge of going to the gym and engaging in regular exercise.

By enlisting the support of a fitness coach and mentor, I have gained valuable guidance and motivation to achieve my fitness goals.

Surrounding Myself with Positive Influences: In seeking to foster a supportive environment, I've connected with positive role models in various spheres of life. Whether through church, community involvement, or new friendships, I've cultivated relationships that accept me for who I am and inspire me to grow.

Incorporating Reflection and Prayer: Recognizing the importance of self-reflection and spiritual guidance, I have integrated moments of reflection into my daily routine. By incorporating prayer points and Scriptures into my reflections, I've found solace and guidance in times of need.

Personal Discoveries and Growth: I have made insightful personal discoveries and experienced significant growth through this journey. Learning to set boundaries and prioritize self-care has empowered me to no longer tolerate disrespect or mistreatment. This newfound sense of empowerment has allowed me to level up and assertively navigate life's challenges.

In each chapter of my story, I offer insights from the lessons I've learned, paired with prayer points, Scriptures, and uplifting messages. This growth journey allows me to reflect, evolve, and gratefully embrace life's blessings.

Hindsight: Lessons learned

Engaging in a deep reflection activity, I pondered over the intricate connections between trauma and certain behavioural patterns. Victims of trauma often find themselves predisposed to being people-pleasers, a tendency that stems from a deep-seated need for validation and approval. This inclination can be traced back to childhood experiences of neglect or abuse, where the individual learned to prioritize others' needs over their own to avoid further harm or conflict.

Similarly, the phenomenon of victims of trauma being drawn to abusive relationships is a complex interplay of psychological factors. In many cases, individuals who have experienced trauma may gravitate towards abusive partners due to a warped sense of familiarity or a subconscious belief that they deserve mistreatment. This destructive pattern of behaviour often perpetuates a cycle of abuse, further entrenching the individual in a cycle of trauma and dysfunction.

Amidst these challenging dynamics, the question arises: is there such a thing as a perfect marriage for children to learn from? As I delved into this question, I reflected on my own dreams and aspirations. From a young age, I harboured a deep longing for the idyllic fairytale wedding, envisioning a life filled with love, children, and boundless happiness. My goal was to provide my future children with the nurturing, supportive environment I yearned for but did not receive during my upbringing.

With this vision, I dreamed of raising my children to the highest standard possible, showering them with love, care, and protection. I wanted to break the cycle of trauma and dysfunction and create a legacy of healing and wholeness for future generations. In doing so, I hoped to provide my children with the foundation they needed to thrive and flourish in their own lives.

As I engaged in this reflection activity, I realized the profound impact that my own experiences of trauma had on my aspirations for the future. Through introspection and self-awareness, I gained a deeper understanding of the complex interplay between trauma, relationships, and the pursuit of happiness. Armed with this insight, I was determined to chart a new course for myself and my family, one defined by inner strength, healing, and pursuing true fulfilment.

Time to reflect

Imagine dreaming of your perfect fairytale wedding, having amazing children, raising them to the highest standard possible. Then waking up one day to find your dream busted by life's unexpected twists and turns. What would you do differently with the benefit of hindsight?

(If I had known that .....   I would have done ...... and saved myself untold grief and anguish.)

Write a letter to your future self; explain some of the hotspots to look out for to avoid getting entangled in a potentially turbulent relationship.

NOTES

Chapter Eleven: *Sharing Our Lived Experiences*

Mistakes are an inevitable part of our journey and often serve as valuable lessons that shape our growth and development. However, what truly sets individuals apart is their ability to take ownership of those mistakes, learn from them, and empower others through their experiences. When we acknowledge our wrongs and actively work to turn them into lessons, we gain personal growth to inspire and support those around us to do the same. Here are some tips on how to embrace mistakes, take ownership, and empower others through our life experiences:

Acknowledge Mistakes Honestly: The first step in taking ownership of our wrongs is to acknowledge them honestly. Avoid making excuses or shifting blame onto others. Accept responsibility for your actions and recognize the impact they may have had.

Reflect and Learn: Create time to reflect on what went wrong and why. Identify what factors contributed to the mistake and consider what you could have done differently. Use this reflection as an opportunity for personal growth and learning.

Share Your Story: Don't avoid sharing your experiences with others. By being open about your mistakes and the lessons you've learned, you create an environment where others feel comfortable doing the same. Sharing your story can inspire others to confront their challenges and embrace personal growth.

Lead by Example: Take the lead by demonstrating humility, accountability, and bounce-back-ability through mistakes. Show others that it's okay to stumble and fall, as long as you're willing to get back up and keep moving forward.

Offer Support and Encouragement: When others make mistakes, offer them support and encouragement rather than judgment. Share your experiences and lessons learned to help them navigate challenges. Empower them to take ownership of their mistakes and turn them into opportunities for growth.

Celebrate Progress: Celebrate your progress and the progress of those around you. Recognize and acknowledge the efforts of others as they confront their mistakes and work towards positive change.

Stay Resilient: Mistakes are a natural part of life, and setbacks are bound to happen. Stay resilient and use each challenge as an opportunity to learn, grow, and become stronger.

Mistakes are not a reflection of your worth as a person. Instead, they're opportunities for growth and self-improvement. By taking ownership of your mistakes and empowering others through your life experiences, you can create a culture of learning, overcoming with determination, and personal development.

Guide to Nurturing Your Child(ren) Through Life's Realities

Dear Parent/Carer,

In today's world, it's crucial not to shy away from equipping our children with the tools they need to navigate life's complexities. More than any other, this generation requires our candid honesty, enduring love, and unwavering support as they navigate the unpredictable moments that shape their future. Here are some mentoring tips tailored to various relationships and situations:

1. For Young Parents: Triggers to Look For

Pay attention to your emotional responses when interacting with your child.

Notice patterns of behaviour that evoke strong reactions, as these may be triggers from your own past experiences.

Seek support from mentors or therapists to work through these triggers and develop healthier coping mechanisms.

2. Hidden Messaging/Secrets – Don't Tell

Encourage open communication with your child to create a safe space for sharing thoughts and experiences.

Teach the importance of honesty and integrity, emphasizing that secrets can harm relationships and lead to distrust.

Model transparency in your own interactions to show that it's okay to discuss difficult topics openly and respectfully.

3. Community Leaders and Family Members

Create a sense of community and respect for elders and authority figures in your child.

Encourage learning from the wisdom and experiences of those around them.

Teach them to seek guidance and support from trusted adults while empowering them to make their own decisions.

4. *Internet Influence [Hiding Unsavory Behaviours]*

Educate your child about online safety and the risks of engaging in harmful activities online.

Monitor internet usage and establish clear boundaries and expectations for online behaviour.

Encourage open dialogue about their online experiences and address concerns together.

5. *Training Your Child About the Facts of Life*

Approach discussions about sensitive topics with honesty, empathy, and age-appropriate language.

Create a safe and non-judgmental environment for these conversations, allowing your child to ask questions and express their feelings.

Provide accurate information and dispel any myths or misconceptions they may have.

6. *Fear of Revealing and Fear of Consequences*

Validate your child's feelings of fear and reassure them that it's natural to feel apprehensive.

Emphasize honesty and integrity, while also acknowledging that mistakes happen and can be learning opportunities.

Work together to explore coping strategies for managing fear and facing consequences with tenacity and courage.

7. Call Centres and Child Helplines

Educate your child about support services like helplines, and call centres.

Teach them how to access these resources in times of need for practical assistance, emotional support, or guidance.

Emphasize the importance of seeking help when facing difficult situations, reassuring them that support is available.

By implementing these mentoring tips, parents can nurture healthy relationships, open communication, and strength in their children as they navigate life's challenges and transitions.

Time to reflect

Who do you know that needs the guidance tips shared in this raw and honest book?

Share my story with them by sending them the link to this book. Let's join hands to impact every individual seeking lasting healing and transformation.

Thank you.

Chapter Twelve: *Healing Prayers*

In our journey through life, we encounter various challenges that test our strength, faith, and resilience. Whether it's the stress of daily responsibilities, personal struggles, or moments of doubt, it is crucial to find solace and rejuvenation through prayer, Scripture, and positive affirmations.

This collection of healing prayers, Scriptures, inspirational quotes, and affirmations will help you connect with God, find inner peace, and build deeper self-love and gratitude.

Gratitude and Faith

Prayer Points:

1. Thank the Almighty for your life and your positive actions.

Lord, I thank You for the gift of life. Help me to recognize and appreciate the positive steps I take each day.

I will praise You, for I am fearfully and wonderfully made; marvelous are Your works, and that my soul knows very well. (Psalm 139:14)

2. ***Express gratitude for open communication with friends and family.***

Thank You, God, for the open and honest communication I share with my friends and family. May we continue to support and understand each other.

Let each of you look out not only for his own interests, but also for the interests of others. (Philippians 2:4)

3. ***Appreciate your pastor, prayer meetings, friends' or community members' willingness to join in prayer.***

Lord, I am grateful for my pastor, prayer meetings, and the friends and community members who join me in prayer. Strengthen our faith and fellowship in Jesus' Name.

And let us consider one another in order to stir up love and good works, not forsaking the assembling of ourselves together, as is the manner of some, but exhorting one another, and so much the more as you see the Day approaching. (Hebrews 10:24-25)

Gratitude for Relationships and Support

Prayer Points:

1. ***Thank God for your friends' positive impact on your life.***

Thank You Lord for my friends who bring me joy and support. Bless them and our relationships in Jesus' Name.

A friend loves at all times, and a brother is born for adversity. (Proverbs 17:17)

2. ***Express gratitude for the love and support from your family.***

Thank You, God, for my family's love and support. Help us to grow closer and stronger together in Jesus' Name.

Honor your father and your mother, that your days may be long upon the land which the Lord your God is giving you. (Exodus 20:12)

3. ***Appreciate the guidance and wisdom of mentors in your life.***

Lord, I am grateful for the mentors who guide and inspire me. Bless them with wisdom and strength in Jesus' Name.

Where there is no counsel, the people fall; but in the multitude of counselors there is safety. (Proverbs 11:14)

Gratitude for Personal Growth and Opportunities

Prayer Points:

1. ***Thank God for personal growth and development.***

Lord, I thank You for the personal growth and development I am experiencing. Continue to mould me into the person You want me to be in Jesus' Name.

But grow in the grace and knowledge of our Lord and Savior Jesus Christ. To Him be the glory both now and forever. Amen. (2 Peter 3:18)

2. ***Express gratitude for opportunities to serve and help others.***

Thank You, God, for the opportunities to serve and help others. Use me as a vessel of Your love and grace in Jesus' Name.

As each one has received a gift, minister it to one another, as good stewards of the manifold grace of God. (1 Peter 4:10)

3. **Appreciate your skills and talents.**

Lord, I am grateful for the skills and talents You have given me. Help me to use them for Your glory.

For we are His workmanship, created in Christ Jesus for good works, which God prepared beforehand that we should walk in them. (Ephesians 2:10)

Gratitude for Faith and Spiritual Growth

Prayer Points:

1. **Thank God for your faith and relationship with Him.**

Lord, I thank You for the faith You have given me and for our relationship. Help me to grow closer to You each day.

For by grace you have been saved through faith, and that not of yourselves; it is the gift of God. (Ephesians 2:8)

2. **Express gratitude for the Bible and its guidance.**

Thank You, God, for the Bible and the guidance it provides. Help me to understand and apply Your Word in my life.

Your word is a lamp to my feet and a light to my path. (Psalm 119:105)

3. **Appreciate your church community's fellowship and support.**

Lord, I am grateful for the fellowship and support from my church community. Bless our unity and spiritual growth.

For where two or three are gathered together in My name, I am there in the midst of them. (Matthew 18:20)

Gratitude for Life and Relationships

Prayer Points:

1. **Thank God for life and the positive actions you take.**

Heavenly Father, thank You for the gift of life. Help me to recognize and appreciate the positive steps I take each day.

I will praise You, for I am fearfully and wonderfully made; marvelous are Your works, and that my soul knows very well. (Psalm 139:14)

2. **Appreciate your pastor, prayer meetings, and your friends' or community members' willingness to join in prayer.**

Lord, I am grateful for my pastor, prayer meetings, the friends and community members who join me in prayer.

Father, strengthen our faith and fellowship by Your grace.

And let us consider one another in order to stir up love and good works, not forsaking the assembling of ourselves together, as is the manner of some, but exhorting one another, and so much the more as you see the Day approaching. (Hebrews 10:24-25)

3. **Be grateful for your family's love and support.**

Thank You, God, for my family's love and support. Help us to grow closer and stronger together.

Honor your father and your mother, that your days may be long upon the land which the Lord your God is giving you. (Exodus 20:12)

4. **Appreciate your mentors' guidance and wisdom.**

Lord, I am grateful for the mentors who guide and inspire me. Bless them with wisdom and strength.

Where there is no counsel, the people fall; but in the multitude of counselors there is safety. (Proverbs 11:14)

5. **Thank the Almighty for personal growth and development.**

Lord, I thank You for the personal growth and development I am experiencing. Mould me in Your Image.

But grow in the grace and knowledge of our Lord and Savior Jesus Christ. To Him be the glory both now and forever. Amen. (2 Peter 3:18)

6. **Appreciate your skills and talents.**

Lord, I am grateful for the skills and talents You have given me to serve others. Help me to use them for Your glory.

As each one has received a gift, minister it to one another, as good stewards of the manifold grace of God. (1 Peter 4:10)

For we are His workmanship, created in Christ Jesus for good works, which God prepared beforehand that we should walk in them. (Ephesians 2:10)

7. **Thank God for your faith and relationship with Him.**

Lord, I thank You for the faith You have given me and for our relationship. Help me to grow closer to You each day.

For by grace you have been saved through faith, and that not of yourselves; it is the gift of God. (Ephesians 2:8)

Chapter Thirteen: *Morning Devotion and Gratitude Affirmations*

Level Up Time

Starting the day with gratitude is crucial for resetting the mind for success. Daily devote intentional time to seek God's will and quiet your mind. These prayers, Scriptures and affirmations have greatly impacted my spiritual and emotional well-being.

Benefits of Early Morning Prayers

Increase time management and focus

Allow more time for other tasks

Start each day with positive energy

Seek daily spiritual guidance

Enhance self-discipline and self-love

Morning Prayer

Father Lord, thank You for waking me up today. I'm in awe of Your love, encouragement, and light. Daily shine upon my path in what You want me to pursue.

I'm grateful for Your help in resolving the challenges I faced yesterday. Today I celebrate You and Jesus' birth who died on the cross to save us all and forgive our sins.

Thank You for creating me perfectly in every aspect, for Your purposeful intentions, for life and breath to accomplish Your plan today.

Lord, I seek Your continued strength, wisdom, and courage to keep rising each day to celebrate You, me, and the universe. Loving Father, fill my cup so I can support others. Thank You for another wonderful day. To God be the glory, Amen.

Daily Gratitude

I am grateful for life and my family's good health.

I am grateful for my work and life journey.

I am grateful for every blessing God gives me.

I am grateful for the inner healing and joy that have transformed my children and me.

I am grateful for the friendships and immense support within the workplace and other nurturing relationships.

I am grateful for my Vicar and loving, compassionate relationship with God.

I am grateful for the gifts of wisdom, understanding, and discernment.

What other gifts are you grateful for? Write them below.

Affirmations

I am strong.

I am wise.

I am a winner.

I am confident.

I am beautiful.

I am skilled.

I am great.

I am a mirror.

I am a warrior.

I am a fighter.

I am a queen.

I am a daughter of the Most High God.

I am sensible.

I am hard-working and persevere for the best results.

I am patient and kind.

I walk in God's wisdom.

I forgive myself and release every lie from my life.

I am joyful and reflect the life of God within me.

I am worthy to be loved, cared for, and forgiven.

I inspire other mothers, women, daughters, and sons.

I am a shining light that radiates love, care, and compassion to others.

I am comforting, caring, and loving toward my children, myself, and my spouse.

I am divinely guided to achieve my best.

I am bold, blessed, hopeful, and uniquely made.

I am grateful for my good health, sound mind, and positive thought process.

Focus Scriptures

Proverbs 4:23. *Keep your heart with all diligence, for out of it spring the issues of life.*

Matthew 5:8. *Blessed are the pure in heart, for they shall see God.*

1 Peter 3:10. *For 'He who would love life and see good days, let him refrain his tongue from evil, and his lips from speaking deceit.'*

Proverbs 3:5-6. *Trust in the Lord with all your heart, and lean not on your own understanding; in all your ways acknowledge Him, and He shall direct your paths.*

Exodus 13:17-18. *Then it came to pass, when Pharaoh had let the people go, that God did not lead them by way of the land of the Philistines, although that was near; for God said, 'Lest perhaps the people change their minds when they see war, and return to Egypt.' So God led the people around by way of the wilderness of the Red Sea. And the children of Israel went up in orderly ranks out of the land of Egypt.*

Proverbs 3:7. *Do not be wise in your own eyes; fear the Lord and depart from evil.*

Proverbs 16:9. *A man's heart plans his way, but the Lord directs his steps.*

Proverbs 16:25. *There is a way that seems right to a man, but its end is the way of death.*

Matthew 18:3. *Assuredly, I say to you, unless you are converted and become as little children, you will by no means enter the kingdom of heaven.*

Proverbs 21:24. *A proud and haughty man—'Scoffer' is his name; he acts with arrogant pride.*

Prayer Points

Apply these prayers in your daily routine to empower your mind, focus and spirit.

Gratitude for a New Day

Lord, thank You for waking me up and blessing me with a new day, good health, and my family. Thank You for protecting, loving, and covering us with the Blood of Jesus. Thank You for our home and all the big and small things You provide daily. Thank You for my job and all my work colleagues, and the wisdom and confidence You have restored in me. Thank You for the women's group I have found and the gifts of sharing and working together through various topics. Thank You for creating me to become the daughter, child, mother, and wife You intended me to be. Thank You for providing me with the tools and people I have met and those I will meet in the future who will work alongside me to fulfil Your purpose. Thank You for bringing us together as a family. I am forever grateful and humbled by Your love, Lord in Jesus' Name.

Thank You

Thank You, Lord, for restoring peace in my life. Thank You for the courage, wisdom, and hard work I am putting towards my work. Gracious God, thank You for Your presence and protection surrounding me. Father, I am grateful for Your lovingkindness and all the wonderful people You have brought into my life. Thank You for giving me a clear mind and a clean heart. Dear God, thank You for filling my heart with gratitude.

Thank You for the food, clothing, and shelter You have given us. Thank You for my motherhood, the beautiful children You have blessed me with, and the fantastic gift of life. Thank You for guiding me to do what is always best for me and our children.

Gratitude Thermometer Prayers

Thank You, Lord, for the strength, courage, and wisdom You daily instil in me. I feel invincible, loving, kind, and have so much to give to others, my children, work colleagues, and the people around me. I am gifted, talented, awesome, beautiful inside and out, and wonderfully made. I am a patient listener, and always obedient to the Holy Spirit. I am confident and hold no grudge or bitterness towards anyone who has wronged me. I am a forgiving child of God. I am not perfect; I make mistakes like any other person. I embrace correction and learn from mistakes. I am a Queen, I am a child, I am a woman, I am a daughter, I am a niece, I am an auntie, I am a grandchild, and I AM AMAZING!!!

Prayer for Renewal

Father Lord, I feel renewed and confident that today will be phenomenal. Thank You for keeping me awake after the alarm went off this morning and giving me the strength to join in the meeting. Thank You for every learning experience and the lovely people You have brought my way. Father Lord, help me to confidently use the affirmations, gratitude, and prayer tools throughout my day. Teach me to be a prayer warrior and spend time with You.

Thank You for every experience that has moulded me into the courageous person who affirms Your love and comfort. Thank You, my shield of protection, for anointing and guiding me with love. Father, thank You for leading me through the correct unseen doors for my wonderful family and friends.

Prayer for Family Protection and Guidance

Lord, thank You for protecting my family this year. As I journey into the new year, Lord, take away all my fears and sadness. Lord, please guide me in what I need to do. I know by Your grace and the Holy Spirit's power all will be well in the mighty Name of Jesus. You have wonderfully made me and given me plenty of love to share with all my family. Continue to mold me into the person You want me to become.

I am courageous and wise and will not give up easily in any unbearable situations I face as I know You are beside me. I am a good mother to my children; I love and care for each one and pray for their well-being, success, protection, good health, and long life. Lord, I am worthy of all good things in life. Lord, I know every item I have brought to Your table in prayer will materialize in Your perfect time. I am victorious and rejoice in Your Word every day. Lord, I am immensely grateful for the journey You have guided me through to arrive where I am today. Amen.

Every moment you get is a gift; wrap it gracefully.

Chapter Fourteen: *Emotional Healing Quotes*

Joyce Meyer Quotes on Self-Love, Self-Esteem, and Accepting Yourself

Self-Love

You cannot have a positive life and a negative mind. — Joyce Meyer, *Battlefield of the Mind: Winning the Battle in Your Mind*

Learn to love yourself right where you are and you will be amazed at the success you begin to experience in your life. — Joyce Meyer, *Approval Addiction: Overcoming Your Need to Please Everyone*

Self-Esteem

You have been created in the image of God, which means you are amazing just the way you are. — Joyce Meyer, *The Confident Woman: Start Today Living Boldly and Without Fear*

God's approval is the only approval you need, and once you believe that, your self-esteem will begin to rise. — Joyce Meyer, *Approval Addiction: Overcoming Your Need to Please Everyone*

Accepting Yourself

When you accept yourself, you don't need others to accept you. — Joyce Meyer, *Beauty for Ashes: Receiving Emotional Healing*

We all need to grow, but accepting ourselves is the first step toward being the best we can be. — Joyce Meyer, *The Confident Woman: Start Today Living Boldly and Without Fear.*

You cannot have peace until you embrace inner peace. (Joyce Meyer)

Dear God, grant me access to the peace You have given me in my spirit. Teach me how to walk in the Spirit, not in the flesh.

Famous Quotes on Overcoming Trauma

Maya Angelou

You may not control all the events that happen to you, but you can decide not to be reduced by them. — Maya Angelou, *Letter to My Daughter* (2008).

Brené Brown

Owning our story can be hard but not nearly as difficult as spending our lives running from it. — Brené Brown, *The Gifts of Imperfection: Let Go of Who You Think You're Supposed to Be and Embrace Who You Are* (2010).

Haruki Murakami

And once the storm is over, you won't remember how you made it through, how you managed to survive. You won't even be sure whether the storm is really over. But one thing is certain. When you come out of the storm, you won't be the same person who walked in. That's what this storm's all about. — Haruki Murakami, *Kafka on the Shore* (2002).

Viktor E. Frankl

When we are no longer able to change a situation, we are challenged to change ourselves. — Viktor E. Frankl, *Man's Search for Meaning* (1946).

Rumi

The wound is the place where the Light enters you. — Rumi, as cited in Coleman Barks' translation, *The Essential Rumi* (1995).

Oprah Winfrey

Turn your wounds into wisdom. — Oprah Winfrey, as cited in Janet Lowe's *Oprah Winfrey Speaks: Insights from the World's Most Influential Voice* (1998).

Nelson Mandela

The greatest glory in living lies not in never falling, but in rising every time we fall. — Nelson Mandela, *Long Walk to Freedom: The Autobiography of Nelson Mandela* (1994).

Louise Hay

You have the power to heal your life, and you need to know that. We think so often that we are helpless, but we're not. We always have the power of our minds... Claim and consciously use your power. — Louise L. Hay, *You Can Heal Your Life* (1984).

Let these quotes encourage you to overcome trauma, as you reflect on the resilience and strength of the human spirit.

Chapter Fifteen: *Navigating Life's Purpose*

The moment we are born we are filled with a divine purpose, yet our journey often feels bewildering, lacking clarity. Along this intricate path, we encounter numerous challenges and obstacles, each presenting trials and tribulations. However, perseverance and unwavering faith can enable us to conquer these hurdles in the most remarkable ways.

How do we navigate this enigmatic journey and emerge victorious? Through the Holy Spirit's indwelling power, a divine presence that guides and protects us unconditionally. With each step forward, we are guided by an Inner Compass that leads us toward our destined purpose, shielding us from harm and illuminating the path ahead.

In moments of doubt and uncertainty, we must remember to keep pressing forward, trusting in the divine plan woven into the very fabric of our being. We are called to fulfil a unique and irreplaceable role in our gifted existence.

But why am I that person? This question lingers in the recesses of my mind, prompting me to delve deeper into the mysteries of my existence. As I reflect on this inquiry, I am reminded of the countless moments of synchronicity and divine intervention that have shaped my journey thus far. Each triumph and every setback testify to the universe's intricate design, affirming my inherent worth and purpose.

Ultimately, the answer to why I am that person may sometimes elude me. Knowing that I am exactly where I am meant to be, guided by a Higher Power who knows the deepest longings of my soul fills my heart with great joy and contentment.

I choose to stand tall and embrace an independent mind, bold career, and an unwavering spirit. I have journeyed through the depths of pain and emerged transformed, uniquely robed in grace and righteousness. This final stage is about my liberation. I am free to move forward, uniquely and powerfully. I am anchored in the strength of my womanhood, fully embracing my self-worth and the freedom to define my own path.

My resilience and determination to break the cycle of abuse testify to my strength and offer hope for others. By God's grace, I have chosen to rise above the odds, embodying the diversity and power of what it means to be a woman who will not be defeated.

This is my message to the world—especially to young people and women: I can overcome, I can thrive, and I am a force for change.

As I continue to grow, I know that true strength lies in my independence and the richness of my connections. I embrace the beauty of building deep, meaningful relationships with my children, community, and everyone I encounter.

I desire to inspire others to see their worth, believe in their ability to transform, and understand that they too can rise healed and empowered.

As a resilient woman, I exemplify the meaning of living free, whole, and fully alive. As I continue journeying forward, empowered with faith and conviction, I embrace life's unfolding mysteries and trust the Divine plan that awaits.

I champion the rights and well-being of individuals across the gender spectrum, including females, non-binary, and binary individuals, alongside boys and girls of all sexes. My mission is to promote awareness and understanding surrounding grooming and sexual abuse in all its forms.

I am determined to reach out to remote villages in Africa, Asia, North America, Europe, and Australia, where access to education and resources may be limited. Through outreach programs and community initiatives, I aim to empower residents with knowledge and tools to recognize and prevent instances of grooming and abuse.

In addition to community outreach, I advocate for comprehensive education on these critical issues within schools, churches, and households. Equipping students, congregations, and domestic staff such as drivers, nannies, and cooks with the necessary tools and knowledge, can help us create safer environments and empower a culture of vigilance and support.

Useful Resources for Support

List of useful organisations, agencies, and helplines for survivors of child sexual abuse, child abuse, trauma, suicide, single parenting, and incest:

Child Abuse & Sexual Abuse Support

NSPCC (National Society for the Prevention of Cruelty to Children)
Website: www.nspcc.org.uk
Helpline: 0808 800 5000
Email: help@nspcc.org.uk

Childline (Support for Under 19s)
Website: www.childline.org.uk
Helpline: 0800 1111 (24/7)

The Survivors Trust
Website: www.thesurvivorstrust.org
Helpline: 08088 010 818
Email: info@thesurvivorstrust.org

One in Four (Support for Survivors of Sexual Abuse)
Website: www.oneinfour.org.uk
Helpline: 0208 697 2112
Email: admin@oneinfour.org.uk

Rape Crisis England & Wales
Website: www.rapecrisis.org.uk
Helpline: 0808 802 9999

NAPAC (National Association for People Abused in Childhood)
Website: www.napac.org.uk
Helpline: 0808 801 0331
Email: support@napac.org.uk
Suicide & Crisis Support

Samaritans (24/7 Emotional Support & Suicide Prevention)
Website: www.samaritans.org
Helpline: 116 123 (Free, 24/7)
Email: jo@samaritans.org

CALM (Campaign Against Living Miserably – Support for Men)
Website: www.thecalmzone.net
Helpline: 0800 58 58 58

Shout (24/7 Crisis Text Line)
Website: www.giveusashout.org
Text: SHOUT to 85258

Trauma & Mental Health Support

Mind (Mental Health Support)
Website: www.mind.org.uk
Helpline: 0300 123 3393
Email: info@mind.org.uk

Rethink Mental Illness
Website: www.rethink.org
Helpline: 0808 801 0525

Survivors UK (Support for Male Survivors of Sexual Abuse)
Website: www.survivorsuk.org
Helpline: 0203 598 3898
Email: help@survivorsuk.org
Single Parents Support

Gingerbread (Support for Single Parents)
Website: www.gingerbread.org.uk
Helpline: 0808 802 0925

Family Lives
Website: www.familylives.org.uk
Helpline: 0808 800 2222

VISION BOARD

My Vision Board: A Path to Fulfilment

Allow me to share with you the story behind my vision board, crafted with purpose and passion to guide me on my journey towards achieving my dreams. When I embarked on the mission of writing a book, I needed a visual representation to anchor my aspirations and keep me focused on my goals.

I set out to create my vision board by reflecting on the experiences and challenges that have shaped my life's trajectory. Each trial and triumph served a purpose, leading me to this moment where I stand, alive and filled with a clear sense of purpose by the grace of God, ready to share my story and extend a helping hand to others.

In the centre of my vision board, I placed a photo of the world, symbolizing my aspiration to reach every corner of the globe, touching lives across continents, ethnicities, and religions. Beneath it, the South African flag represents my deep connection to my birthplace and my commitment to making a difference in my homeland.

Moving outward, I included images that inspire and motivate me towards my goals. Oprah Winfrey, a beacon of inspiration, reminds me of the power of storytelling and the impact it can have on others. I aspire to emulate her influence and one day engage in a meaningful dialogue with her.

Adjacent to Oprah, I envision an epic book launch, a celebration of my journey and a testament to the support of friends and allies who stand by my side. The prospect of turning my story into a film fills me with excitement, and I am eager to explore avenues for cinematic adaptation.

Beneath these aspirations lie dreams of returning to Africa, establishing roots, and contributing to my community. I envision traveling the world, promoting my book, and engaging with diverse audiences to spread the message of hope and empowerment.

Above all, my vision board represents my unwavering faith and determination to see my dreams come to fruition. This roadmap for the future guides me toward fulfilling my purpose.

In the journey ahead, I recognize the importance of seeking support and guidance from those around me. When experiencing trauma, their wisdom and compassion can offer solace and strength, nurturing emotional healing and growth.

Looking ahead to the future, I anticipate a year of transformation and opportunity. Open doors, new beginnings, and a deepening sense of self-worth await, propelling me to achieve my goals with courage and persistence.

With an action plan in place, including avenues for book promotion, collaborations, and community engagement, I am ready to embark on the next chapter of my journey. Together, let us embrace the possibilities that lie ahead and turn our dreams into reality.

Time to reflect

Create a vision board of what you desire your life to look like five years from today.

What are five *must-haves* you've always wanted for yourself? Your family? Your education, physical, spiritual, relationships, emotional?

What experiences will help you achieve your *life worth living* feeling? Write it all down then find or create pictures that connect with your vision.

Life isn't static—it's fluid, ever-changing, and full of twists and turns. Sometimes, we feel stuck, but the truth is, we're never truly trapped in one moment or situation. We evolve, we adapt, and we grow. The key lies in knowing which tools to reach for when life calls for them.

Conclusion

Has it been easy? Not at all. Thankfully, I've got to where I am now, but I've stumbled plenty along the way. That's just part of the journey; I'm far from perfect. But what's been great is the range of options I have now, tools, journaling, and prayer have been most helpful.

Learning I am enough in my worth has grounded me; I am content and fulfilled in my purpose.

By God's grace, my children are all thriving in their careers. Bella, a successful lawyer, has partnered with a few colleagues to set up her law firm. Living in a nearby town enables her to come home for a cooked meal and quality time with the family.

Jess, an incredible dancer, is flourishing in theatre productions in New York. I visit her often to watch her shows. Mai lives in Canada, where she runs an art gallery alongside her diplomatic duties. Jack, CEO of his civil engineering firm, plans to create a new city somewhere in Africa.

And my vision board? It's still a work in progress, but I've made some amazing strides. My book launched at different venues to reach diverse audiences. I've also teamed up with a few organizations to host village talks with translators, educating the poor and needy about key topics like grooming, incest, and where to seek help when needed.

My current mission is to build and support educational centres for children and youths in the remote parts of my childhood village where I grew up.

The recently launched podcast has attracted large audiences. Figuring out how to break into the movie industry has proved more challenging, but I'm determined to keep pushing forward.

I'm happier, wiser, stronger, and more courageous than ever. Above all, I'm humbled and grateful to be a role model to many who have experienced heartbreak. I hope that reading this book has inspired you and helped you begin your healing process. What's next in store? Connect with me to discover more.

About The Author

The author is a blessed mother of four beautiful, God-fearing children. Educated with a MSc and BA (hons), she is passionate about fitness, personal well-being, supporting the elderly, alongside helping those in need.

Quick favour: Would you help me connect with readers who would be encouraged and uplifted by the insights shared in **Trauma to Transformed: Uncovering the Gems Within?**

Please share this book's ISBN 9798317257248 with your friends, family, and colleagues to enrich their well-being and spread awareness that hope and healing from emotional and spiritual wounds are available to all.

Leave your best review on Amazon with a brief comment on a fantastic breakthrough you have received from reading this book. You may also add a photo to enhance your review.

May God enrich your life and relationships going forward. Thank you!

Charlotte

References

Angelou, Maya. *Letter to My Daughter*. New York: Random House, 2008.

Brown, Brené. *The Gifts of Imperfection: Let Go of Who You Think You're Supposed to Be and Embrace Who You Are*. Center City: Hazelden Publishing, 2010.

Frankl, Viktor E. *Man's Search for Meaning*. Boston: Beacon Press, 1946.

Hay, Louise L. *You Can Heal Your Life*. Carlsbad: Hay House, 1984.

Lowe, Janet. *Oprah Winfrey Speaks: Insights from the World's Most Influential Voice*. Hoboken: John Wiley & Sons, 1998.

Mandela, Nelson. *Long Walk to Freedom: The Autobiography of Nelson Mandela*. Boston: Little, Brown and Company, 1994.

Meyer, Joyce. *Approval Addiction: Overcoming Your Need to Please Everyone*. New York: Warner Faith, 2005.

———. *Battlefield of the Mind: Winning the Battle in Your Mind*. New York: Warner Faith, 1995.

———. *Beauty for Ashes: Receiving Emotional Healing*. New York: Warner Faith, 1994.

———. *The Confident Woman: Start Today Living Boldly and Without Fear*. New York: FaithWords, 2006.

Murakami, Haruki. *Kafka on the Shore*. New York: Knopf, 2002.

Rumi. *The Essential Rumi*. Translated by Coleman Barks. San Francisco: HarperOne, 1995.

The Holy Bible, New King James Version®. Copyright © 1982 by Thomas Nelson. Used by permission. All rights reserved.

Printed in Great Britain
by Amazon